PEOPLE PERFORMANCE & BUSINESS PLANS

A Guide for the Small Business

By Tom Kennedy, BComm,FCA.

People Performance and Business Plans

Tom Kennedy, BComm., FCA.

Thomas Kennedy is a Fellow of the Institute of Chartered Accountants in England and Wales. He has over thirty years practical experience in business including Business Planning and Control and Performance and Reward.

This book is in presentation format and is designed to help you to align Business Planning and People Performance Management.

People Performance and Business Plans

PEOPLE PERFORMANCE & BUSINESS PLANS

ISBN: 978-1-4116-4662-9

FOREWORD

Most of my career (c 30 years) was spent in a Multi-National environment. In these environments there are sufficient resources including IT Systems, use of large Consulting Organizations plus 'in house' specialized Staff Functions to do things well in the constant struggle to achieve World Class Practices.
In these Organizations there is sufficient scale and resource to ensure that 'the best way to do it in theory' is implemented, suitably adapted, in practice.

However, in recent years in my role as independent consultant, I have found myself mentoring small leadership teams in small to medium size environments. Frequently they ask for advice as their enterprises grow and

FOREWORD cont'd…

need to acquire more formalized structures.

This book arose from consultancy work for the Chief Executive of a small IT company. As the company expanded rapidly the CEO wished to understand how the business should be planned and how these plans should be communicated to the individuals in the organization. In particular the CEO wished to link the rewards for individuals to their achievement and contribution in relation to the Business Plan.

People Performance and Business Plans

INTRODUCTION

The big picture

Today's World

Successful Small Businesses

Conflict resolution

Introduction

Sometimes it is hard to get the big picture.

For you the big picture may be yourself or you and a partner and maybe with a couple or a few co-workers running around chasing your tails making a living.
You may be fighting hard to stand still. You may be bigger and getting organized for growth and further success.

You will have to scale this book to fit to your business; it is not one size fits all.

What is it? It is the right way to do thing
Introduction cont'd...You may have to adapt the scale to your resources, but if

Introduction cont'd...

you adopt the principles of the approach it should be what you need.

 You may be the boss who started small and now has a mixture of staff in support. It may seem that the Finance people slave away in their corner of the business and the Human Resources Guys are immersed in whatever it is they do and you wonder are they a necessary evil or can they add value?

Every business has a bottom line. It must make money, generate cash flow, grow or die, change or be changed.

The people in the business make the difference. Their attitudes and values drive how the business interacts with the world.

Introduction cont'd…

What I have done in this book is to set out a view of the Business Planning Process and the People Performance Process and how the two should tie in together.

I hope this will be useful to the Chief Executive or Senior Manager who is trying to grow a successful small business.

My hope is that you get good ideas for the way forward in your business.

Introduction cont'd

IN Today's World:

INFORMATION IS KEY

MARKET DISTANCES ARE VANISHING

ACTIVITIES, NOT JUST PRODUCTS, ARE SOLD

THE RISE OF KNOWLEDGE WORKER LEADS TO
   DIFFERENT EXPECTATIONS

CUSTOMERS EXPECT CONVIENIENCE & RESPONSIVENESS

CONSTANT CHANGE IS NORMAL

You know this and you know the business you are in. To survive and grow you must be competitive and able to change and flex to the market place.

Introduction cont'd

Consider, what are the critical success factors in your business…?
Write a short list in the notes page at the back of this guide. Check on yourself as you read on.

Introduction cont'd

Successful Small Businesses
In my experience the following are critical for success:

HAVE PRODUCT /SERVICE CLARITY

HAVE CLEAR HIRING CRITERIA (esp… Family/Friends)

HAVE CLEAR MANAGEMENT TRANSITION PLANS (including Entrepreneur exit strategy and shareholder exit strategy)

HAVE CLEAR JOB RESPONSIBILITIES

HAVE GOOD RELATIONSHIPS WITH FUNDS PROVIDERS SUCH AS SHAREHOLDERS AND BANKS

COMMIT TO RESOLVING INTERNAL CONFLICTS QUICKLY

Introduction cont'd

Conflict Resolution

Conflict can arise from a number of circumstances and can unnecessarily absorb energy and scarce management time on inward soul searching, taking away from the need to be outward looking and flexible.

In start up situations and in times of difficulty including pace of expansion, shareholders who are investors may want to dabble and even undermine the role of the Chief Executive.

MULTIPLE STAKEHOLDERS WITH POWER CAN LEAD TO:
DIVERGENCE IN GOALS
DIVERGENCE IN SOLUTIONS
CLEARLY THIS IS BAD FOR
BUSINESS

IF NECESSARY USE OUTSIDE MEDIATORS

Introduction cont'd

CONFLICT RESOLUTION CAN BE BY POLITICAL DECISIONS BUT SHOULD BE THROUGH OPENNESS AND COMMUNICATION, LEADING TO BREAKTHROUGH.

You can use the Strategic Review Process set out in this guide to provide a basis of discussion and establish alignment.

It does not matter whether stakeholders are Shareholders, Directors or Employees or Union officials. Open communication, building trust are vital. Outsiders can arbitrate but in the longer term, the team must pull together. If there is a union, they should be kept informed at local level of the needs and threats to the business.

People Performance and Business Plans

Contents of this Guide

We will look at these in turn and set out action plans.

Part one

Internal Frameworks

Clearly performance in the market place determines success and survival.

However if the business is well organized internally and the 'team of employees' are all aligned in the direction the business needs them to be, then there is a sound foundation upon which the business can prosper. In addition to ensure success you want the Company's employees to behave appropriately towards the customer and each other, even when you are not there.
To achieve this certain internal processes must be set up and maintained.

Part one

Internal Frameworks

There are two distinct Frameworks:
We will deal with each in turn and
then show how they interconnect.

The Directional Framework

Who are we? Where are we
going? What will we
become?

The Support Framework

How will we behave? How
are we set up to manage?
Do we have internal self
knowledge and awareness
about the Business?
We deal with this area in
part two.

PART ONE
SETTING THE DIRECTIONAL FRAMEWORK

The components are:

VISION – what will we be?

MISSION – Why do we exist?

STRATEGIC REVIEW

SET STRETCH TARGETS

IDENTIFICATION OF CAPABILITY GAPS

ROUTES TO VISION

PUTTING NUMBERS ON THE VISION

LEVEL OF DETAIL

COMMUNICATION PLANS

ACTION PLANS

Part one
Setting the Directional Framework

Vision: what will we be?

Expresses a Fundamental Aspiration & Purpose

The top team must see the Vision as an expression of their intentions so that they use it as a point of reference in their actions. The top team must communicate the Vision to their reports and on down the organization. Use of public statements, slogans and publicity all help drive awareness of the Vision.

Take the time and space to work together and agree the Vision for the company.

Keep this simple for example 'To be the best at…' Stick to a few sentences maximum.

A clearly understood vision reaches all employees and provides a sense of how the business sees itself in its area of business. It is different from but linked to the Mission

Part one
Setting the Directional Framework

MISSION

WHO ARE WE?

WHAT BUSINESS ARE WE IN?

WHAT ARE WE ABOUT?

The mission must be clarified before proper Strategies can be developed. The mission is defined by way of a process of discussions designed to enable the top team, initially, to share understanding and knowledge of the business they are in and to arrive at alignment in their thinking.
The mission, which will compliment the 'Vision,' can then be communicated to all the organization.
MISSIONS
The mission might be to 'shape the Internet' or to be 'the most innovative...' in that Organizations field of business

Part one
Setting the Directional Framework

Management needs to spend time and money to arrive at agreement around VISION and MISSION for the Business.

Part one
Setting the Directional Framework

The Strategic Review

The objectives of the Strategic Review are to generate long-term plans for the business and to set stretch goals for the medium and long term.
This Review should be undertaken every year as it is very difficult to guess the future and forecasts must be regularly revised.

UNDERTAKE YEARLY AND REVIEW YEARLY

UNDERPIN WITH ANALYSIS:
EXTERNAL ENVIORNMENT
- STRENGHTS/WEAKNESSES
- THREATS/OPPORTUNITIES
- ALLIANCES
- COMPETITION
- MARKET POTENTIAL
INTERNAL ENVIORNMENT
- Assess Capabilities

Use the analysis to assess the potential for the Business.

Part one
Setting the Directional Framework

Strategic review cont'd

SET **STRETCH GOALS** (5 OR 6)
Using the analysis undertaken for the Strategic Review.

The Top Team, probably the board and some key managers, undertakes this work. They come together as a Team to discuss the way forward. Use internal and external resources and sources of intelligence to assist. However the completion of the work must belong to the responsible Director and then, following discussion for clarification and understanding, the way forward should be agreed and owned by the Team

Part one
Setting the Directional Framework

Strategies versus Tactics

It is important not to mix up Strategies
and Tactics
STRATEGIES
LONG TERM PLANS
SURVIVAL/COMPETING
MINIMUM TWO YEARS
ANNUAL REVIEW
WIDER RISKS
TOP MANAGEMENT PLAN
MODERATE DETAIL
TACTICS
MEANS TO IMPLEMENT
SPECIFIC GOALS
ONE YEAR OR LESS
QUARTERLY REVIEW
RISK CONTROL
MIDDLE MANAGEMENT
DETAILED PLAN
Tactical goals are more appropriate to
the Annual Budget cycle when the
budget is broken down into Monthly
and Quarterly targets and action plans.

Part one
Setting the Directional Framework

Long Term Stretch Goals

Avoid analysis paralysis. Uncertainty is normal. When the best possible view is available, act on it. Don't expend too much energy on the last percentage of accuracy. Just be flexible and be decisive and action centred.

In setting Long Term Stretch Goals:

> Use Common Sense.
> People should be able buy into them as practical and achievable.
> They should appeal to the heart as well as the head.
> And Contribute to long-term success.

Goals arising from the Strategic Review should be Strategic Goals. **Limit Strategic Goals to a maximum of 5 or 6 goals** to ensure clarity and manageability.

Part one
Setting the Directional Framework

Identify Capability Gaps

Having set five or six Broad yet stretching Goals it is necessary to review the organization's capability to deliver. Ask the following questions:

*How does the current performance compare with the 'Aspirational Performance' as reflected in the Stretch Goals?

*What gaps exist in capabilities?
> - People expertise? Have we the correct people in the correct slots?
> -Can the product range and the production plant handle the expected future?
> -Can our sales and marketing capabilities match the challenge?

*What gaps need to be plugged in order to make success possible?

Part one
Setting the Directional Framework

Capability Gaps, cont'd

*Is the Organizational Structure capable of handling the level of 'Aspirational Performance'?

-For example are the correct Functions in place?
 e.g. Finance, HR, Product Development.
-For example, are the correct people in the correct roles in the Functions?

*Do we need to reorganize or hire in expertise?

- Is the skill mix suitable for the future?
- What are the gaps in succession plans?

(see also the section 'Support Structure' that follows below.)

Part one
Setting the Directional Framework

Routes to the Vision

Having analysed and diagnosed and set
stretch targets and reviewed the
Organizational Capability, it is now
time to flesh out the route to be taken
in achieving the Vision.

To start, as far as possible, put in place
any restructuring and reorganization of
people and roles. Restructuring the
management team to meet future
challenges will send very strong
messages into the Organization.

Develop Broad Strategic Plans
covering the next three to five years.
These plans will be revised every year
to take account of changing realities
facing the business.

Start with three or five year estimates.
The longer the estimate the less
accurate but the need of the business
will dictate how far it is necessary to

Part one
Setting the Directional Framework
Routes to the Vision cont'd…

flesh out a level of broad detail. A particular forecast should be chosen for detailed work up. This can then be flexed as necessary using 'what if?' type scenarios.

The immediate years ahead must be fleshed out in sufficient detail to enable an overview of the business in terms of funds flow, profits as well as sales targets, market share, marketing plans etc.

There must be sufficient numbers in terms of financials, key ratios and timetables to enable achievement to be monitored as the business goes forward. Funding and investment needs must be in sufficient detail to enable discussion with shareholders or banks so that longer-term arrangements can be put in place.

The process to do this is set out in the next two sections.

Part one
Setting the Directional Framework

Putting numbers on the Vision

This process should also be used as a communication exercise, taking the top level work on Vision and Mission and Overall Strategy, with Stretch Targets, down into the business and communicating intent and securing involvement of all key players.

It is important to understand the communication element. It is of vital importance in aligning the efforts of the teams within the business and giving coherence to their activities. Deliberately set out to create discussion and debate, use study/project groups, off site meetings and seek alignment and use the exercise for Team building. Celebrate success.

Part one
Setting the Directional Framework
Putting numbers on the Vision cont'd…

Having decided on the Strategic Plan time frame (3 to 5 years), prepare worked up estimates as follows for the time period selected:

> *Sales Estimates (by product, market etc)
> *Narrative Plans with appropriate key ratios for vital areas such as future Marketing and Sales and Promotion plans.
> *Capital Project requirements to support product volume/mix
> *Cash flow/funding needs/profits

The objective is to produce a costed Strategic Plan.
This Plan is prepared for each significant Function in the Organization.
The Strategic Plan is based around the Sales Forecasts.

Part one
Setting the Directional Framework
Putting numbers on the Vision cont'd...

The first year of this Strategic Plan will provide a basis for the detailed Annual Budget, later on in the planning cycle.

Having prepared figures on the basis of the most likely Sales Forecast, 'What if' scenarios can be calculated around the core estimate and risk analysis can be completed.

The detail necessary is spelt out below.

Part One
Setting the Directional Framework

Detail of the Strategic Plan

Each Function (e.g. Sales, Finance, Production etc)will prepare:

*Short Narrative Plans setting out the key result areas for that Function in achieving the Strategic Plan. This will include key milestones and timings, interdependencies and risk analysis.

*Key numbers and critical success factors expressed as far as possible in numbers and ratios.

*Manning requirements including recruitment or redundancies and training needs.

*Capital Programme Requirements broadly costed for funding but not as a go ahead. (All Capital Projects should be submitted individually for approval as a separate exercise when they are worked up in full detail for approval.)

Part one
Setting the Directional Framework

Detail of the Strategic Plan cont'd...

Each Function must submit their Strategic Plan to the Board for approval.
The approved plan must be costed and put together for the business (by the accountants) to arrive at the bottom line in terms of funds flow, profits etc. A number of iterations may be necessary to get it right. This will involve rethinks, cut backs etc, in a dynamic environment. The relevant section of the agreed plan will be communicated to line managers so they understand what is required of them.

Part one
Setting the Directional Framework

Communication Plan

Secret Plans won't engage the people working in the Business.

Consider who needs to know and what they need to know and how much. The objective in sharing is to enable high performance and to motivate.

Make it clear what areas the employee is expected to keep confidential and from whom.

We will consider this in more detail later under the header 'Engaging the Organization.'

Part one
Setting the Directional Framework

Action Plan for your Directional Framework

In Summary, the Leadership Teams must:

ARTICULATE A VISION

ASSESS THE ENVIORNMENT

SET AND AGREE STRETCH GOALS

DETERMINE THE PERFORMANCE GAP TO BE BRIDGED TO ACHIEVE THE GOALS

DIAGNOSE ORGANISATIONAL PROBLEMS

DEVELOP A STRATEGIC PLAN

PLAN HOW TO MONITOR AND IMPLEMENT

COMMUNICATE, COMMUNICATE, COMMUNICATE

Part two

DEVELOPING THE SUPPORT FRAMEWORK FOR YOUR BUSINESS

Part two continued

Developing the Support Framework

Your Products or Services may be the best thing since the development of the wheelbarrow... ...

BUT...

Your business needs INTERNAL SELF KNOWLEDGE to prosper. This is the Support Framework

Rivals can match technical aspects of your business.
At the end of the day the quality, the capability, the attitudes and the beliefs of the people working in the business are critical to success.

Part two
Developing the Support Framework

The Support Framework consists of:

CULTURE:

The way things are done around here.

VALUES AND BEHAVOURS:

Systems of beliefs practiced and aspired to.

Part two
Developing the Support Framework

The Culture
The 'way things are done around here' is evidenced by:

Appearances
PRACTICES BY LEADERS
NARRATIVES/STORIES
LANGUAGE USED
SYMBOLS OF SUCCESS

Practiced realities
NORMS FOR SURVIVAL IN
THE GROUP
VALUES OF THE GROUP
ASSUMPTIONS AS TO
ACCEPTABLE BEHAVIORS
SOCIALISATION BY PEER
GROUP

Part two
Developing the Support Framework

Culture & Political Correctness

People watch and learn from their peers and their bosses. They distinguish the reality from the aspiration. They will act as they perceive necessary while on the surface they will play the game. They will adopt the best survival behaviors for themselves even if the business has a different outward aspiration.

The point is that if there is a mis-match between the Culture as articulated and communicated and that practiced in reality the individuals in the Company will pick this up. Actions speak louder than words and behaviours inappropriate to the desired culture must be challenged if change is to be achieved.

Part two
Developing the Support Framework

Culture cont'd

Examples of positive Cultures:

PEOPLE ENCOURAGED TO
SOLVE PROBLEMS

PEOPLE TAKE RESPONSIBILITY
AND GET THINGS DONE

TEAMWORK

SUPERVISOR AS ROLE MODEL

WALK THE TALK

FREE AND OPEN
COMMUNICATION

MAKING NEEDED RESOURCES
AVAILABLE

Part two
Developing the Support Framework

Values and Behaviours
underpin the culture

Values:
- Will drive behaviours between employees and employees and between employees and the customer
- May lead to sub cultures in parts of the organization

Developing new Values
- Define the unacceptable ways to do things
- Articulate the Management Operating Style necessary to reflect the culture, values and behaviours desired. Put this in writing.

Part two
Developing the Support Framework

Key Organizational Values

Leadership
High standards
Continuous Learning
Trust
Flexibility
Reward
Recognition
Innovation
Involvement
Partnership

Part two
Developing the Support Framework

DESIRABLE VALUES AND BEHAVIORS

Examples:

Pride - We are the best!

We value our people

Everybody will want to contribute

Recognition -Everyone gets a place in the sun

Coaching and Continuous Learning

Informed workforce

Low standards not acceptable.

Poor performance confronted

Customer focus and flexible external focus

Challenging and responsible jobs.

Part two
Developing the Support Framework

ACTION PLAN FOR YOUR SUPPORT FRAMEWORK

The Leadership Team must understand the importance of creating the right Culture as reflected in Values and Behaviours actually practiced in the Organization.

Inappropriate Management Styles must be challenged and changed or weeded out.

The Chief Executive has a huge influence on the style of the organization and he must accept the need to give appropriate Leadership.

The Organization Structure must be such that is promotes cooperation and teamwork

Part two
Developing the Support Framework
Action Plan for your Support Framework
cont'd...

The Leadership Team must understand the need to have an Organic Organization Design (see below) which of necessity will flex and change with the Organization. Roles are not fixed forever and neither are reporting lines.

Individuals must be helped through retraining and team support, to grow and change with the business.

We deal in more detail with Management Structures in the next part, part three.

Part three

Leadership, Management and Teamwork

Part Three
Leadership, Management and Teamwork

Elements:

- Planned Evolution

- Definitions

- Phases in Business Growth

- Organization Structures

- Leadership

- Management Roles and Activities

- Teamwork

- Building Team Spirit

Part Three
Leadership, Management and Teamwork

Planned Evolution

The Chief Executive must plan ahead of the curve and flex and expand the Organization Structure and put resources in place to enable achievement of the 'Stretch Goals'

He must also monitor current management performance and be prepared to move, sideline or lose poor performers especially at Board Level.

He must mentor and counsel high performers and he must help those who are struggling (and keep proper documentation to record discussions)

Part Three
Leadership, Management and Teamwork

Planned Evolution, cont'd.,

The size of the Organization will be a key influencer and by identifying where the Organization is in terms of scale it will be possible to plan the changes.
WITH SMALL NUMBERS IT IS POSSIBLE TO GRASP EVERYTHING

WITH A WIDER SPAN OF CONTROL DELEGATION IS ESSENTIAL

AS THE BUSINESS GROWS IN SIZE
- Functional Specialists should be allowed to evolve.
- Structured lines of command are needed.

Part Three
Leadership, Management and Teamwork

Some Definitions:

Organizations evolve and go through different phases. Let us understand some definitions.

SPECIALISATION
- a means of assigning tasks

STANDARDISATON
– Uniform Practices and Processes

COORDINATION
- Integration of Task and Process

AUTHORITY
- Right to decide at a specific level

As the Organization grows each of these areas must be examined to establish the appropriate level. Regardless of size **Poor Performers must be confronted, retrained, changed or replaced**.

Part Three
Leadership, Management and Teamwork
Different Phases/ Different Needs
Start up Phase
    Entrepreneurs
    Funds management critical
Development Phase
    Cash management
    Technical product
    Source customers
Growth Phase
    Cash Management/Control
    Systems
    Marketing/Sales/Quality
Maturity Phase
    Profitability/cash flow
    Functional structures
    Need to re-launch/re-energize
    regularly
Comment:
Individuals wishing to survive and prosper with the business must be able to flex and adapt to the changing environment. Through Teamwork individuals can achieve more than the sum of the individuals and help each

Part Three
Leadership, Management and Teamwork
Different Phases/ Different Needs
Comment cont'd.

other change and grow.
Different people (including the Chief
Executive) have skills appropriate to
the different phases of the business.
(see phases above). Individuals must
therefore continue to grow at a
personal level with the business to be
able to continue to make an effective
contribution at each phase of the
business.
The Primary responsibility for
personal growth lies with the
individual. However, the Business, in
enlightened self-interest, should help
the individual to achieve their potential
through mentoring and training.
If individuals cannot move on with the
business they must either be replaced
or their competencies supported by
appropriate recruitment.

Part Three
Leadership, Management and Teamwork

Organization Structure

We referred above in the Section on Strategic Review, to the need to ensure that the Organization Structure is appropriate to the future and that key positions are staffed by individuals with appropriate attitudes and skills to deal with the future and the achievement of the stretch goals set for the Organization.

The structure must cover the bases:

> General management
> Finance
> Product development
> Market development
> Sales
> Production
> Human Resources
> Procurement

Scale drives structure and in a small organization some areas may be combined under one individual to optimize resources

Part Three
Leadership, Management and Teamwork

Leadership

- The Leadership Team sets the tone for the Business
- Anyone who takes responsibility is a Leader
- Delegate and Mentor to grow Leadership competence
- Development may include participation in Cross Functional or Multi-Discipline Task and Project Groups

Attributes for successful Leadership are:

> Visionary
> Confident
> Trustworthy
> Considerate
> Inspirational
> Thoughtful

Leaders make the difference and everyone should be encouraged to give leadership but should also know when it is appropriate to follow.

Part Three
Leadership, Management and Teamwork

MANAGEMENT ROLES:
You should ask:
- Does everyone know their role?
- Are the roles clear and clearly described in writing?
- Are the necessary skills in place to carry out the roles?
- Is a single person accountable for delivery?
- Do we have clarity at to why this role is needed?

MANAGEMENT ACTIVITIES:
You should ask:
- What will a good outcome look like?
- What will be the review process?
- Are there milestones along the way with key responsibilities?
- Are there publicly visible deadline events built in?
- How do we communicate progress during the activity?
- How will we celebrate success along the way?

Part Three
Leadership, Management and Teamwork

TEAMWORK

The members of a Team don't have to be friends (It helps). However they should enjoy working together, be mutually supportive and stimulated by challenge to work together to get results. The individuals in a Team should have sufficient personal/people skills to be able to work and pull together within the Team

- Success requires teamwork within the business
- Teams are committed to pursuing a shared purpose
- They should have the required mix of skills
- They hold themselves accountable for success or failure

A team spirit in an Organization is a major energiser. Developing a 'team spirit' is therefore a key area for attention.

Part Three
Leadership, Management and Teamwork cont'd

EFFECTIVE TEAMWORK. HOW DO YOU GROW A TEAM SPIRIT?

FIRST RELAX AND TRUST IN ORDER TO BUILD TRUST:

- Build an atmosphere that is informal, comfortable and relaxed
- Encourage a lot of pertinent discussion in which everyone participates
- Show respect by being prepared to listen to each other and give every idea a hearing
- Where there is disagreement it is accepted as an expression of a genuine difference of opinion
- Allow a lot of decisions to reached by a kind of consensus

Part Three
Leadership, Management and Teamwork cont'd

Teamwork…
First relax in Order to build trust: cont'd…

- Permit criticism that is honest, open and comfortable and without fear of reprisal or condemnation
- Encourage people to be free in expressing their feelings as well as their ideas, both on the problem an on how the team is operating.
- The boss is the boss but the group does not defer unduly to him or her.

SECOND BUILD CLARITY:

- Ensure that task or objectives of the group is well-understood and accepted by the members

Part Three
Leadership, Management and Teamwork
TEAMWORK...

Second : Build Clarity cont'd…:

- When action is decided, clear assignments are made and accepted
- The group is self aware around it's role
- The group has shared values around the objectives as well as around individual needs
- Have a set process for defining the key priorities
- Ensure that competencies / skills of the group fit the objective
- Deal with issues not personalities

PART FOUR

THE LEARNING ORGANIZATION

Part Four
The Learning Organization

The object is to have a favorable environment in which to foster the right culture and behaviors

This requires us to design:

A Learning organization

With an Organic Design

Part Four
The Learning Organization

The Learning Organization...

...WANTS TO DELIGHT THE CUSTOMER

ATTRIBUTES:

Shared Leadership

Customer Focused Strategies

Intensive use of Information

Culture of Innovation

Flexible and Responsive

Organic Organization Design

Part Four
The Learning Organization

Features of Organic Organization Design

- TASKS INTERDEPENDANT WITH TEAMWORK AND COMMUNICATION

- TASKS CONTINUALLY ADJUSTED TO REFLECT INTERACTION & CHANGE

- RESPONSIBILITY FOR TASKS BEYOND SPECIFIED ROLE

- NETWORKED STRUCTURE OF CONTROL AND COMMUNICATION

- VERTICAL PLUS HORIZONTAL DECISION MAKING

- MUTUAL INFLUENCE AND ADVICE

LIKE AN ORGANISM THE ORGANIC STRUCTURE FLEXES AND CHANGES TO DEAL WITH ITS ENVIORNMENT

Part Four
The Learning Organization

Action Plan for Implementing the Learning Organization

1. ARTICULATE THE REQUIRED CULTURE IN TERMS OF VALUES AND BEHAVIOURS

2. ARTICULATE THE REQUIRED OPERATING MANAGEMENT STYLE TO SUPPORT THE CULTURE

3. ASSESS THE ENVIORNMENT

4. SET AND AGREE STRETCH GOALS

5. DETERMINE THE PERFORMANCE GAP TO BE BRIDGED TO ACHIEVE THE GOALS

6. DIAGNOSE ORGANISATIONAL PROBLEMS AND MAKE CHANGES

7. PLAN HOW TO MONITOR AND IMPLEMENT

8. HOLD REGULAR REVIEWS

9. ENGAGE THE WHOLE ORGANIZATION(See part five)

Part five.

ENGAGING THE WHOLE ORGANIZATION

OR HOW TO DO ALL THIS IN REAL LIFE

Part five
Engaging the whole Organization

The theory is complex and time is precious. A lot of consultants will tell you what you ought to do, what your Organization should feel like, but can be less useful (or too expensive) in helping you to get there in your particular business.

There is no 'One size fits all' solution. The template must be adapted to the needs of your business.
The Chief executive must provide the Leadership to create energy and priority. Hard work by the Management team is the best way forward. They must believe and be involved.

Part five
Engaging the whole Organization
Cont'd.

TRY THIS:

HOME WORK AND HARD WORK

USE IN- HOUSE TEAMS

MAYBE HIRE CONSULTANTS

THEN:

ENGAGE THE WHOLE
ORGANIZATION

Part five
Engaging the whole Organization
Cont'd
COMMUNICATION WITH AND ENERGISING THE WHOLE ORGANIZATION

To achieve alignment is necessary to invest in a communications program to convey what is expected of the whole organization.

The writer George Bernard Shaw is attributed with the quote…

'The problem with communication is the belief that it has been achieved.'

What is needed is relentless communication using all available media including and especially managers walking about out of their offices talking to their reports about what is planned for the organization.

Part five
Engaging the whole Organization
Cont'd

Good quality documentation should be used when setting out the Vision and the Mission.

This in turn connects with the proposed Culture, Values and Behaviors and is reflected in the Management Operating Style. Again high quality documentation should be used to set all this out for all to see and understand.

Part five
Engaging the whole Organization

Action Plan for Engaging the whole Organization

- 'In House' Team established
- Consultants hired (if required)
- Meetings Timetable Set
  Board Level
  Management Level
  To review and agree the planned
  Communication Programme
- Seek alignment with stakeholders such as Associated Companies Suppliers and Customers where necessary
- Implement Communications Plan
  - o Use internal media such as in house publications
  - o Address Union Leaders
  - o Questions and answers sessions with Staff in small groups
  - o Walking about and talking to people
  - o Feedback on queries raised.

Part six

MANAGING PEOPLE PERFORMANCE

Part Six
People Performance

Let us examine these in turn:

Emotional Contracts

Managing Reward:

Principles

Philosophy

Guidelines

Performance Review Process:

Objectives of the process

Managing the process

Action Plan

Part six
People Performance cont'd

Emotional Contracts:

Behaviour is a broad Parish. There are many influences on behaviour. People's individual needs differ and the same individual will have different needs at different ages and at different stages in their lives and in their careers.

Human emotions are complex and interplay at all levels. The written contract of employment is one thing, however individuals bring their feelings to work and interact with their environment on a number of emotional levels.

The best Environment can be created by driving an agenda around Culture, Leadership and Performance.

Part six
People Performance cont'd

People must adapt to and work within the Organization's Culture. At the end of the day individuals have the primary responsibility to develop their own skills and competences and their careers within the Organization. The Organization should act with enlightened self-interest to facilitate the individual's progress. Let us consider the Emotional Contract between the Individual and the Organization.

Part six
People Performance cont'd

EMOTIONAL CONTRACTS

PEOPLE HAVE A WRITTEN
CONTRACT OF EMPLOYMENT

BUT THE REWARDS FROM
WORKING COME FROM A
NUMBER OF COMPLEX
SOURCES:

LIFESTYLE
     THE SOCIAL ENVIORNMENT
     LIFESTYLE BALANCE
     CARING ENVIORNMENT
WORKSTYLE
     WORKING RELATIONSHIPS
     RISK SHARING
     FREEDOM
     AUTONOMY
     PACE OF WORK

Part six
People Performance cont'd
EMOTIONAL CONTRACTS cont'd…

QUALITY OF WORK
    PERCEIVED VALUE OF THE
    WORK
    ACHIEVEMENT
    CHALLENGE
    RECOGNITION
    WORK INTERESTING
FUTURESCOPE
    IMPROVED
    EMPLOYABILITY
    CAREER ADVANCEMENT
    LEARNING AND
    DEVELOPMENT
    IMPROVEMENT
    FEEDBACK ON
    PERFORMANCE
TANGIBLES
    PHYSICAL ENVIORMENT
    SUSTAINABILITY OF
    EMPLOYMENT
    WORK FACILITIES
    JOB SECURITY

Part six
People Performance cont'd
EMOTIONAL CONTRACTS cont'd...

MONEY
    MARKET RATE
    MARKET BENEFITS
    FAIRNESS OF PAY DEAL

PEOPLE WILL DECIDE TO STAY
OR GO BUT THE BUSINESS
SHOULD HAVE A WORKED UP
UNDERSTOOD REWARD
PHILOSOPHY WHICH
REGOGNISES THE TANGIBLE
AND THE INTANGIBLE
ELEMENTS SET OUT ABOVE.

Part six
People Performance cont'd

MANAGING REWARD

Reward is just one of several closely interrelated platforms for the management of what is now called Human Resources, meaning the people who work in the Organization. These platforms are:
*Organization Development which covers Change Management, Leadership Development, Talent, training and mentoring together with succession planning.
*Employee Relations which deals with Industrial Relations, Health and Safety, Equality Legislation
*Resourcing including recruitment, promotion manpower planning
*Organization Structures which cover the alignment and specialisation of resources to accomplish the tasks of the Organization in a structured manner.

Part six
People Performance cont'd
MANAGING REWARD cont'd

Reward supports these HR platforms and seeks to optimise performance. The first step is to develop a set of reward principles and a supporting reward philosophy.

Part six
People Performance cont'd
MANAGING REWARD cont'd

Reward Principles

Reward should reflect the following features:

Support other HR Platforms

Support Business Strategy including innovation and growth

Convey messages about the values and expectations of the Organisation.

That the Philosophy and practices will be developed as far as possible with involvement of Line Managers and employees including full discussion of concerns arising.

Part six
People Performance

MANAGING REWARD cont'd

Reward Philosophy

Examples:

Financial Rewards are seen as a key enabler and driver of performance.

Rewards will be differentiated according to individual performance, skill and competence, and reflect the value placed on the role by the Company.

Reward levels will be sensitive to market forces.

Rewards will reflect the success of the business.
Equity should be seen to exist within and across job families.

Performance rewards structures may differ (e.g., Sales -v- Admin) according to business needs.

**Part six
People Performance cont'd**

Reward Philosophy cont'd...

Within the scope of overall equity and budget, Line Management should decide pay levels.

Change is a continuous reality and the reward structures should be responsive and flexible enough to deal with ongoing change.

Part six
People Performance cont'd

Reward Philosophy and Individuals

Individuals must know what is expected of them but note:

What is measured is what will be quantifiable

What is used to assess performance will get attention

Avoid conflict between team/business objectives and individual Key Result Areas (KRA's)

Individuals should be entitled to request a review of any decision on their pay and grade.

Part six
People Performance cont'd
Reward Philosophy and Individuals cont'd…

Individuals should have some choice on the benefits they receive.

Managing Change is part of the day job

Individuals should have the clear right to access the boss of their immediate boss

Individuals should have confidential access to the Human Resources Function to discuss problems and seek advice on future development.

Pay should not be seen as an exclusive motivator and suitable processes need to exist to facilitate non-financial motivators.

Part six
People Performance cont'd
MANAGING REWARD cont'd

Reward guidelines:

Base pay covers the rate for the job size and will reflect both the ability of the individual and the market rate for the job.

The Organization policy may be to pay the average of market rate or a higher percentage, e.g to pay in the upper quartile on average. The Organization may also have a policy around market rate for example, to pay 80% for beginners and say not more than 120% to highly competent experienced individuals who the Organization feels it needs to retain.

Bonus can be linked to individual performance and or to either Organizational Performance at macro level or divisional level.

Part six
People Performance cont'd
Reward Guideline cont'd...

The Bonus Scheme should be
understood by those operating it and
by those participating.
Bonus can be an amalgam of
Individual Performance and
Organizational Performance.
Bonus schemes can be devised and
tailored to different groups for
example Sales force or Senior
Managers.
Bonus schemes can be short/medium
term e.g. sales targets, or long term,
e.g. business growth or share price.

Clearly bonus schemes can provide a
link to the Business Plan when targets
are set using the Business Plan.

The targets should be appropriate to
the group being bonused.

Part six
People Performance cont'd
Reward Guideline cont'd...

Bonus scheme design should be careful to avoid

-Equality Legislation issues

-Payment for results not within the control of the bonus - groups, e.g. good weather or population trends.

-Switching off or dis-incentivise other groups

-Inflexible exclusive focus on the targets

In general it is good news if a bonus scheme pays out. However, the scheme should not be part of pay and conditions and should therefore be capable of being abandoned if Management do not like the outcomes.

Part six
People Performance cont'd
Reward Guideline cont'd...

Benefits packages should reflect market practice and the organization's retention policies. For example, pension provision may be seen as necessary in the employment market both to attract the right individuals and to retain them once recruited.

Part six
People Performance cont'd

The Performance Review Process

OBJECTIVES for The Annual Performance Review

Objectives in relation to Individual Performance Review
*To communicate to the individual his line managers view of the individual's performance.

This includes Team-work, commitment, attitudes, willingness and other relevant personal traits. The Review should cover the individuals Operating Style and whether it fits to the Culture and desired Operating Style for the Organization.

*To agree with the individual the extent to which personal goals and targets have been achieved.

95

Part six
People Performance
The Performance Review Process
Objectives in relation to Individual Performance
Review cont'd

*To agree with the individual the extent to which targets derived from the Business Plan and agreed for that Individual, have been achieved.

*To communicate results that will influence bonus payments related to personal performance.

*To discuss individual training and development needs

Part six
People Performance
The Performance Review Process

Objectives in relation to Organizational overview

*To provide a fair method of acknowledging performance in different areas of the business.

*To gather data on training needs

*To manage career development

*To identify high performers and address their training and development needs

*To align individual targets with Business Plan Targets in a clear measurable way

*The Managing Board and Chief Executive should recognize the vital importance of the Management and Development of performance

Part six
People Performance

Managing the Performance Review Process

Board meetings should be scheduled with an agenda to discuss and agree:
(Based on data provided by HR and Finance)
In advance of the Annual Performance Review

- Outcomes of the Strategic Plan and Budget exercises and implications for local targets and key priorities.
- The criteria around good or bad or very good performance, so that board members have a consistent and agree in approach that can be communicated down line.
- Timings and schedules for the Performance Reviews and be aligned on giving line managers the time to do this well.

- Performance of individuals considered high performers and how these are perceived in other areas of the business. Again the objective is to achieve consistency and alignment around what is considered to be high performance.

After the exercise.

- Across Function statistics showing how ratings vary from average in each Function. This is to form a view on the consistency with which the exercise has been completed.
- To agree base pay guidelines and bonus calculations
- Fit to training budget

Part six
People Performance
Managing the Performance Review Process

After the exercise cont'd

- Talent and proposed development for agreed individuals
- Poor performers and their future

Part six
Part six
People Performance
Managing the Performance Review Process

Points:

Link to Business Plans so as to ground the process in reality

You gct what you pay for. If you want more you must appeal to the heart as well as the head.

Plant and processes can be copied but people make the difference. Investing in people is the road to success

A clearly understood calendar sets the framework (See section on Timetables for Planning and Control)

The Human Resources Function, who will supply guidelines and standard formats to record the discussions, should coordinate the process. Both the assessor and the individual whose

Part six
People Performance
The Performance Review Process
Managing the Performance Review Process
Points cont'd

performance is being appraised should
sign the documentation.

Part six
People Performance
The Performance Review Process
Managing the Performance Review Process
cont'd

THE PROCESS should be open and Understood

To measure a person's performance it is necessary to decide on the criteria against which that performance will be measured.

To ensure a fair system of assessing performance across the Organization a systematic approach, coordinated by the Human Resources Function is required.

There should be as far as possible a clear line of sight for the individual between the individual's reward outcomes and that individuals personal performance.

Part six
People Performance
The Performance Review Process
Managing the Performance Review Process
cont'd

The Process TAKES TIME

Ideally Performance assessment should be continuous but most managers find it difficult to sit down monthly and do a review.

If quarterly performance targets have been set this provides a mechanism for at least a quarterly review.

However an annual assessment is too late for poor performance. There should be no major shocks at annual assessment the individual should have a good idea of what the Boss thinks from previous conversations.

It is essential that poor performance is confronted when it is evident. Conversations should take place and the situation should not be allowed to fester until it is exposed at an annual performance review.

Part six
People Performance

ACTION PLAN FOR PEOPLE PERFORMANCE

1. ARTICULATE THE REQUIRED CULTURE IN TERMS OF VALUES AND BEHAVIOURS

2. ARTICULATE THE REQUIRED OPERATING MANAGEMENT STYLE TO SUPPORT THE CULTURE

3. TRANSLATE THE STRATEGIC PLAN AND ANNUAL BUDGET IN PERFORMANCE PROMISES FOR EACH AREA OF THE BUSINESS. THESE ARE EXPRESSED IN TARGETS AS HARD NUMBERS, MILESTONE TIMINGS, KEY RATIOS AND KEY RESULT AREAS.

Part six
People Performance cont'd
Action Plan for People Performance cont'd…

4. THIS PROCESS IS TOP DOWN, TARGETS FOR HEAD OF FUNCTIONS BEING BROKEN OUT INTO TARGETS FOR AREAS AND FOR INDIVIDUALS.

5. THE INDIVIDUAL SITS DOWN WITH HIS MANAGER AND DETERMINES INDIVIDUAL KEY RESULT AREA AND OBJECTIVES. THESE WILL SUPPORT THE ACHIEVEMENT OF THE MANAGERS TARGETS AS REFLECTED IN THE BUSINESS PLANS

6. MANAGER AND INDIVIDUAL AGREE HOW TO MONITOR AND IMPLEMENT AND WHEN TO HOLD REGULAR REVIEWS

Part six
People Performance cont'd
Action Plan for People Performance cont'd…

7. CARRY OUT A MAJOR ANNUAL PERFORMANCE REVIEW EXERCISE AND FOLLOW UP WITH BOARD LEVEL DISCUSSIONS ON THE OUTCOMES

8. FOLLOW UP ON TALENT DEVELOPMENT

9. FOLLOW UP ON MANAGEMENT OF POOR PERFORMANCE.

10. SET GUIDELINES FOR ANNUAL PAY AWARDS

11. AGREE BONUS CALCULATIONS

Part seven

TIMETABLES FOR PLANNING AND CONTROL

Part seven
Timetables for Planning and Control

We will examine:

- Coordination using a Planning Cycle
  - o Features of the Planning Cycle

- Business Calendars
  - o For Financial Planning
  - o For Financial Feedback
  - o The Human Resources Calendar

- Action Plan for Calendar Management

Part seven
Timetables for Planning and Control

We have described :
- The Directional Framework and the associated Business Plans
- The Support Framework for setting the Climate and Operating Style
- Leadership and Organizational Structures for the Business
- People Performance and the links to pay and reward.

These are complex exercises and must be worked within the resources available to the Organization. Even if the full detail set out and described in the preceding pages cannot be followed due to resource and manpower limitations, the principles set out must be adhered to, so as to set the business on the right pathway forward.

Part seven
Timetables for Planning and Control

Co-ordinating these exercises requires hard work, but also requires a timetable for the year so that it all fits together.

Part seven
Timetables for Planning and Control

Coordination using a Planning cycle.

PLANNING CYCLE FEATURES:

A CONTINOUS FEEDBACK LOOP - between what is actually happening on the ground and what is going on in the Planning Process.

APPROPRIATE COMMUNICATION - to those responsible for achieving Objectives and targets

CALENDAR OF EVENTS - to specify where the process should be at any particular point in time.

INDIVIDUAL ROLES IN PROCESS UNDERSTOOD for example, a Manager undertaking an Annual Performance review.

Part seven
Timetables for Planning and Control
Planning Cycle Features cont'd

CALENDER PUBLICISED so individuals know what is scheduled for when.

Part seven
Timetables for Planning and Control
Planning Cycle Features cont'd

Business Calendars

There are a number of Business Calendars or Timetables. These are co-ordinated to ensure Business Plans are linked into the People Performance Management Process:

- The Financial Planning Calendar
- The Financial Feedback Calendar
- The Human Resources Calendar

Part seven
Timetables for Planning and Control
Business Calendars cont'd…

THE FINANCIAL <u>PLANNING</u> CALENDER

START OF YEAR - STRATEGIC REVIEW
DISCUSSIONS AND POSITION PAPERS, with
Marketing and Sales scenarios and proposed capital
expenditures over three to five years

DURING FIRST QUARTER- develop COSTED
STRATEGIC PLAN with Objectives/Capex,
Funding, Manning, Three years of Profits/Cash
flows

MID YEAR TO THIRD QUARTER
- Prepare ANNUAL BUDGET with Key
Performance Indicators (KPI)'s, Profits, Capital,
Cash and Monthly Budgets/targets for coming year

Part seven
Timetables for Planning and Control
Business Calendars cont'd...

THE FINANCIAL <u>FEEDBACK</u> CALENDER

START OF FINANCIAL YEAR
Actual results for the previous year, in terms of Financials, key Ratio's, become available during the first month.

MONTHLY ACCOUNTS
Revenues, Costs & Capital Expenditure. The actual results as they roll out each month.

REPORTS AND REVIEWS
Project progress at key milestone dates for Major Capital Projects and Study Groups

BUDGET REVISIONS (Profit/cash Re-estimates)
Quarterly and Final Estimate in last quarter.

The outcomes of actual events are continuously fed back into the future planning process. Link first year of long term plans into the Annual Budget

Part seven
Timetables for Planning and Control

The Human Resources (HR) Calendar
This Calendar links to the Financial Calendars set out above

The Financials - both results and plans are fed into the Annual Review System for Performance Appraisal.

This is done by setting Individual Targets, Key Ratios and Critical Success factors that are linked to and derived from :

- The Strategic Plan and Annual Budgets.

- The requirements around Culture and Operating Style

Undertake Quarterly updates to flex targets based on actual results achieved.

The ANNUAL REVIEW- is held in first quarter of the New FINANCIAL Year.

This is a formal documented meeting.

If quarterly mini-reviews have taken place during the year there should be no sudden surprises at the year end review.

Part seven
Timetables for Planning and Control
The Human Resources (HR) Calendar cont'd...

It is difficult to find the time to do interim reviews but they are highly desirable. In particular poor

performance should be targeted and dealt with in advance of the year-end.
If a poor appraisal is expected the individual should be given advanced notice by holding documented coaching sessions during the year.

The Annual Review **looks backwards** to Cover Performance, Pay Review Bonus, and Awards.
It provides a clear line of sight, connecting pay review and bonus outcomes to Performance in terms of measurable, achieved objectives.

- Discussion of performance based on previous years results
- Discussion around Operating Style and Teamwork

The Annual Review also **looks forwards** because it:

- Incorporates future Business Targets as Objectives for the coming year.
- Covers Personal Development Targets for the coming Year. Includes Operating Style and Team Behaviours.
- Covers Training needs, Career aspirations.

Part seven
Timetables for Planning and Control

ACTION PLAN FOR CALENDAR MANAGEMENT

LETS' TIE IT ALL TOGETHER

THE BUSINESS NEEDS GROWTH AND IMPROVED PERFORMANCE.

WE TACKLE THIS THROUGH STRATEGIC PLANS, IDENTIFYING KEY RESULT AREAS AND ESTABLISHING GROWTH PLANS AND PERFORMANCE PROMISES.
These Business Plans include not only the numeric targets, but also the pathways to realise the Vision and Mission of the Business and the required Support Structures around Culture, Behaviours and Operating Style.

IN TURN THESE ARE CONVERTED INTO BUDGETS AND ACTION PLANS.

BUDGETS ARE BROKEN DOWN INTO AREAS OF RESPONSIBILITY.

PROGRESS IS MONITORED THROUGH A FEEDBACK LOOP TO ACTUAL FINANCIAL RESULTS AND PROJECT PROGRESS REPORTS.

Part seven
Timetables for Planning and Control
LETS' TIE IT ALL TOGETHER cont'd...

**AT THE START OF THE YEAR, AS PART OF
THE ANNUAL REVIEW, THE INDIVIDUAL
SITS DOWN WITH HIS MANAGER THEY
DETERMINE INDIVIDUAL KEY RESULT
AREAS AND OBJECTIVES FOR THE YEAR
AHEAD**

THESE INDIVIDUAL OBJECTIVES
- **Are drawn from and support
  achievement of the Manager's area of
  responsibility as reflected in Strategic
  Plans and Budgets.**
- **They may include Team Objectives
  that are common for all the
  individuals on the team, but are
  specific to the expected contribution
  from the individual.**
- **They will include Operating Style and
  Behaviours consistent with the desired
  Business Culture.**

**THE MANAGER UNDERTAKES REGULAR
REVIEWS WITH THE INDIVIDUAL TO
ASSESS PERFORMANCE AND TO
MONITOR PROGRESS ON INDIVIDUAL
DEVELOPMENT NEEDS.**

**DEVELOPMENT MAY INCLUDE
PARTICIPATION IN CROSS-FUNCTIONAL
OR MULTI-DISCIPLINE PROJECT AND
TASK GROUPS.**

Part seven
Timetables for Planning and Control
LETS' TIE IT ALL TOGETHER cont'd…

THERE SHOULD BE NO SURPRISES AT THE ANNUAL REVIEW MEETING, AS PROBLEMS SHOULD HAVE BEEN IDENTIFIED AT THE REGULAR REVIEWS, WHICH CAN BE MONTHLY OR QUARTERLY.

ONCE A YEAR THERE SHOULD BE A FORMAL DOCUMENTED CONVERSATION BETWEEN THE MANAGER AND THE INDIVIDUAL TO UNDERTAKE A PERSONAL DEVELOPMENT REVIEW AND TO DISCUSS CAREER DEVELOPMENT OPPORTUNITIES.

PROGRESS ON COMITTMENTS MADE AT THIS MEETING WILL BE FOLLOWED UP AT THE REGULAR REVIEW MEETINGS ABOVE.

THE INDIVIDUALS ACHIEVEMENTS WILL BE REFLECTED IN HIS/HER TOTAL REWARD AND RECOGNITION PACKAGE:
> **PAY LEVEL AND PAY AWARD**
> **BONUS CALCULATION**
> **BENEFITS IN KIND (COMPANY CAR, MEDICAL INSURANCE, PHONES, TRIPS ETC)**
> **RECOGNITION AND NON-FINANCIAL INCENTIVES**
> **SUPPORTED CAREER DEVELOPMENT AND TRAINING**

Part seven
Timetables for Planning and Control
LETS' TIE IT ALL TOGETHER cont'd...

Where recognition of Performance and Achievement is assessed and measured against targets derived from Business Plans this process will ensure alignment of efforts towards the priorities of the Organization.

Performance and the associated Reward must be linked to key Business Targets to ensure coordinated effort across the Organization.

NOTES:

NOTES:

NOTES:

NOTES:

People Performance and Business Plans